The Neutra

The Neutrality of the Soul

"The Neutral Soul
Reckons the Old-man Dead to Sin"

James A. Brettell, DMin

Brettell Publishing
Maumelle, Arkansas

Copyright © by Rev. Dr. James A. Brettell

All rights reserved. No part of this publication may be reproduced, stored in a retrieval system, or transmitted in any form or by any means, electronic, mechanical, photocopying, digital, recording or otherwise without prior written permission of the author.

ISBN-13: 978-1461132950

To my friend Gary Johnson who raised the question in my Monday Night Home Bible Study regarding who reckoned the old-man dead to sin; and then to Al Rosenblum, Steve Ellis, and all of the Sunday evening Webex meeting participants without whom the answer to Gary's question would not have been pursued. Thanks to Ed Halsband for proof-reading the manuscript.

Romans 6:11

Likewise reckon ye also yourselves to be dead indeed unto sin, but alive unto God through Jesus Christ our Lord. (KJV)

ABOUT THE AUTHOR

Dr. James A. Brettell, born in Mingo Junction, Ohio, November 2, 1934, graduated Mingo Junction High School in 1952, worked for the Pennsylvania Railroad, the F.B.I., played professional baseball in the Pittsburgh Pirate system, and served nine years in the United States Navy as a Hospital Corpsman. He earned All-Navy recognition for pitching two baseball no-hitters within four days, and pitched in the "world series" finals of military baseball in 1957. He was stationed in Guantanamo Bay, Cuba, during the "Castro revolution" and stationed in Trinidad during the Cuban missile crisis. He was saved at age 27 while stationed at the U.S. Naval Station, Trinidad, W.I. His academic background is diverse. He studied at George Washington University, College of Steubenville, Kent State University, Akron University, Oklahoma University, Southwestern Baptist Theological Seminary, Luther Rice Seminary, and University of Arkansas at Little Rock. His earned degrees: B.S. in Ed. from Akron University; MDiv and DMin from Luther Rice Seminary. His pastorates: North Maple Baptist Church, Stuttgart, Arkansas; South Highland Baptist Church, Little Rock, Arkansas; Bible Doctrine Church of Little Rock; Bible Doctrine Church of the Deaf; and presently pastors the Little Rock NetChurch. He has made twenty missions trips to Mindanao, and two to Seoul, Korea. He has been a Youth Camp speaker and has hosted an annual Arkansas Winter Family Retreat. He has hosted several of his own radio programs and a television program. He hosts a ninety minute daily radio program, a Monday Night Home Bible Study, Little Rock NetChurch Sunday morning worship services and Sunday evening Webex meeting. He has streamed ten "live" video services a week to the internet. His first published book is titled, *"Christianity in Spiritual Perspective: Are You Sick-and-Tired of Being Sick-andTired?"* He has been married to Janet Shawhan Brettell since 1956 and has three adult children, four grandchildren, and one great-grandchild.

Contents

Dedication	iii
Epigraph	iv
About the Author	v
Preface	vii
Text	1
Introduction	1
Terminology	1
Establishing Some Concepts	10
Where It All Started	11
Does the New-man Reckon the Old-man Dead to Sin?	11
Does the Old–Man Reckon the Old-Man Dead to Sin?	15
The Old-Man Is Reckoned Dead by the Neutral Soul	15
Introductory Information That Builds a Solid Foundation	16
More Foundational Information	20
What Is Meant by Wanting-to-Want	24
The Believer and God the Father's Will	26
The Holy Spirit's Role in This Process	34
Who Reckons the Old-man Dead to Sin?	41
One More Time	44
Addendum #1	45
A Bit of Reasoning Amplified	45
Addendum #2	47

Preface

Purpose of This Booklet

This booklet is written as a sequel to this author's first book, *Christianity in Spiritual Perspective: Are You Sick-and-Tired-of-Being-Sick-and-Tired?* Its purpose is to demonstrate how the neutral soul interacts with both the sinful body and the Holy Spirit who indwells the human spirit. It will address such questions as who or what reckons the old-man dead to sin? What is meant by wanting-to-want? What role does the Holy Spirit have in the function of the born-again Christian's life? A significant terminology section is provided to establish the basis for clear communication. A conclusion will be drawn regarding who or what reckons the old-man dead to sin.

Narrative and Outline

This booklet is written in both narrative and outline form. The author believes that if the reader is to be edified spiritually, both forms are important to the subject matter under consideration. The narrative portion lends itself to inductive reasoning while the outline portion lends itself to deductive reasoning. As you study the content of this booklet, please accept both forms as they contribute to your spiritual edification.

Anticipate Redundancy

Redundancy of thought will be encountered throughout the booklet. This is intentional, and not intended to impugn the intelligence of any reader. It's the author's purpose to provide as much information as possible to make clear his immediate line of reasoning, rather than requiring the reader to have to reflect back in the booklet to something previously stated that may not be common knowledge. Thank you for your thoughtful consideration when you encounter redundancy.

Target Groups

Status Quo. This booklet will not appeal to those who are satisfied with the status quo.

Pastors. This booklet will appeal to pastors whose spiritual heart is hungry for something more than "we'll never know until Jesus comes."

The Sick-and-Tired Church-goers. If you can't get your answers from the pulpit, where can you get them? If you want to know how the human soul and human spirit work, you may find your answer in this booklet.

The Church Dropouts. This booklet will appeal to some who have already dropped-out of church, yet still believe that the truth is out there somewhere. The Holy Spirit will lead them to this booklet where they will find *some* answers to the questions they have about the human spirit and human soul.

God knows. This booklet will appeal to those being prepared by God through the circumstances of life. He knows who they are. He can lead them to this booklet that will lead them to Him.

Read or Study?

This booklet is designed for study. To merely read it will make the reader aware of its content, but its purpose will be missed. Read it prayerfully after having asked God the Father to give you clarity of understanding of the meaning of its content.

Concerning Terminology

A terminology section has been provided for the purpose of assisting the reader with an understanding of this author's thoughts. "Too technical," you say?

Perhaps you have not been completely prepared by the circumstances of your life to ask the questions this booklet will answer – and that's okay. We're on God's time schedule, and He's not in a hurry.

Words are symbols used to communicate. If the words being used are not understood by the reader, the purpose for communication has failed; hence, the need for a terminology section.

The terminology used in this booklet is associated with biblical concepts, and it really isn't necessary to agree on the terminology used. Others may desire to use different terms to discuss biblical concepts; however, while disagreement on terminology may exist, it's the concept and its meaning that's important, not the term used. Change the terminology if you must, but let's not change the biblical concept associated with the term.

The Neutrality of the Soul

Text: Romans 6:11

Likewise reckon ye also yourselves to be dead indeed unto sin, but alive unto God through Jesus Christ our Lord. (KJV)

This verse contains the concept of twice reckoning. The second reckoning is elliptical, meaning that it is not stated, but understood as though it were stated. Twice reckoning is noted in the following expanded version of this verse.

Likewise reckon ["reckon^1"] ye also yourselves to be dead indeed unto sin, but ["reckon^2" ye also yourselves] alive unto God through Jesus Christ our Lord. (KJV)

Introduction

This booklet is designed to answer the following question: Who reckons the old-man dead to sin? Is it the old-man or is it the new-man that does so? The answer is neither. It's the NEUTRAL soul, specifically the soul's neutral self-consciousness that makes the decision to reckon the old-man dead to the sinful nature.

Yes, the soul is neutral, and if the soul is neutral, then all of its parts are neutral. Therefore, to discuss any part of the soul is to imply the fundamental neutrality of that part: the neutrality of self-consciousness; the neutrality of volition; the neutrality of mentality; the neutrality of emotion; and the neutrality of conscience.

Terminology

It may be customary to place a terminology section near the end of a book, but the author believes that due to the nature of the content that follows, it is necessary to place a terminology section at the beginning. His reasoning? If the terminology section is placed at the beginning of the book, the reader will have a frame of reference for terminology encountered, and a quick return to this section will refresh the mind regarding the term under consideration.

This booklet, like most of what this author offers, requires more than just reading. The content is not presented as easy reading, but thought provoking information associated with the Christian's spiritual life that is not comprehended using a paradigm based upon an old-man belief system. The believer will learn the truths contained in this booklet only when simultaneously confessed up-to-date and desiring the sincere milk of God's Word. Are you positioned spiritually to learn? Take a moment to examine yourself? Do you have any unconfessed sins in your life? If so, pause for a time of confession. Are you really seeking truth with an open mind? If so, you are ready for this booklet.

Let's begin by considering some terminology that you will encounter in the pages ahead. The terms are listed in alphabetical order. Also note carefully the occasional superscript numbers [1 and 2]. These superscript numbers are designed to show the location of data in the soul's mentality from the time it enters the mentality until it is applied.

back-burner truth: The author uses this phrase to refer to data received by the believer who is clean before the Lord and wanting-to-want absolute truth, but doesn't understand[2] at reference center[2] what the human spirit has transmitted back to reference center[2]. (See the explanations below regarding the words with superscript numbers.) The author recommends that the believer not dismiss this data because it is not immediately understood[2], but recommends that it be permitted to remain on the "back-burner" of the soul's mentality (actually, reference center[2]) until such time as illumination comes. The point? Don't dismiss truth just because you don't immediately understand it. Place it on the back-burner of your mentality.

believe[1]: This term is associated with reference center[1] and understanding[1]. When data enters reference center[1] through the ear gate, eye gate, or tactilely, and is understood[1], the question arises as to whether what is understood[1] is also being believed[1]. If the answer is, yes, this is what is meant by believe[1]. However, it is possible to understand[1], and not believe[1]. For example, if I say to you, "The moon is made out of green cheese," followed by, "Do you understand[1] me?" Suppose you do understand[1]. Now, I ask, "Do you believe[1] what I said?" and you respond, "I understand[1] what you said, but I don't believe[1] what you said." You understand[1] that I said that the moon is made out of green cheese, but you reject that information as inaccurate; therefore, you understood[1] what I said, but did not believe[1] what I said – and rightfully so.

believe[2] – This term is associated with reference center[2] and understanding[2]. When data enters reference center[1] through the ear gate, eye gate or tactilely, and is understood[1] (known[1]), if the data received is *absolute truth*, and if the born-again believer is clean before the Lord, that is, being confessed-up-to-date and simultaneously "wants-to-want" truth, that data immediately advances from reference center[1] into the human spirit wherein the Holy Spirit resides. It is now the Holy Spirit's responsibility as part of His divinely decreed job description to bear witness with the born-again believer's human spirit. He bears witness with the human spirit by teaching the human spirit the meaning of the absolute truth that was received into the human spirit. (Here's an important point. If the data received into reference center[1] through the ear gate, eye gate, or tactilely, is distorted truth rather than being absolute truth, that data will never advance to the human spirit. It is important to understand that word NEVER. Only absolute truth advances to the human spirit.) When the Holy Spirit teaches the human spirit the *meaning* of absolute truth, the human spirit transmits back to reference center[2] the *meaning* of the truth taught. Now that the *meaning* has been transmitted back to reference center[2], the question remains regarding whether self-consciousness will believe[2] what the Holy Spirit has taught. Maybe it will and maybe it won't. There is no guarantee that just because the Holy Spirit has given divinely decreed *meaning* to absolute truth that self-consciousness is going to believe[2] what the Holy Spirit has taught. Please, do not just yet criticize self-consciousness for its unbelief. There is a legitimate reason why it may disbelieve at the moment. (See "understanding[1]" and "understanding[2]" and "application . . ." on pages 7-9 for the explanation of this unbelief.)

confession: Confession is the Greek word ο (μολογεω (homologeo). It is a legal term that means to name, to cite, to identify, and it is found in 1 John 1:9. Confession is a form of prayer to God the Father during which time the believer names any and all *known* sins that he or she has committed since his or her last time of confession. Confession is always addressed to God the Father whose plan it is that has been violated. Confession results in immediate forgiveness and cleansing. When all known sins have been confessed, God the Father not only forgives the *known* sins that have just been confessed, but He also forgives and cleanses every *unknown* sin or sins that could not be confessed because they were unknown (didn't know that what was done was considered sin by God the Father). God the Father treats *forgotten* sins as unknown sins. When the believer has confessed all of his or her known sins committed since the last time of confession, the believer is said to be "clean before the Lord."

confessed-up-to-date: This is the believer's spiritual condition of being clean before the Lord because he has confessed all known post-salvation sins since the last time he had a time of confession. It is the spiritual condition of being able to stand before God the Father experientially forgiven and cleansed of all known and unknown post-salvation sins.

data: This term refers to any information coming into reference center[1] through the ear gate, eye gate, or tactilely. As self-consciousness becomes aware of anything happening in the believer's periphery, self-consciousness passively permits that information to be processed into the mentality's reference center[1]. Do not try to make more out of the word *data* than data being a reference to self-conscious awareness of the events occurring in a human being's life. An event may be something thought, felt, tasted, touched, heard, or seen. It could be an awareness of something directly and immediately affecting the believer or it might only be something happening in human history about which this believer is aware. If the believer trips and falls on the street, self-consciousness is aware of an immediate event that directly involves the believer. However, self-consciousness can also be aware of a catastrophic tsunami in Japan that has no immediate or direct affect on this believer. This is what is meant by the term *data*.

launching center: The launching center is the term used for the location in the soul's mentality that stores data that is ready for immediate application to a life situation. When a life situation triggers an application, whether it's an old-man or new-man application, that application is made (launched, applied) from what is referred to as the launching center.

launching center amplified: The launching center has two platforms from which to apply data to a life situation:

- a conscious platform.
- a subconscious platform.

The conscious platform is the platform from which a conscious decision is made for the purpose of making an application to a life situation.
The subconscious platform is the platform from which an application is made to a life situation without making a conscious decision to make the application. This is referred to as an habituated application.

launching center's conscious platform: The conscious platform is used in early childhood before old-man strategies have become habituated. As a child is learning what "works" to achieve pleasure and prevent pain, when he or she believes[1] (trusts, accepts) a learned strategy, it is stored in reference center[1] and immediately processed to the "conscious platform" of the launching center. It goes to the conscious platform because it has not yet been habituated. When confronted with a circumstance, self-consciousness looks to reference center[1] to determine whether a frame of reference exists for the circumstance. If a frame of reference exists, self-consciousness then turns to the conscious platform and makes the decision to make application of the strategy that equates to the strategy matching the frame of reference. As this particular strategy is applied again and again, it processes to the subconscious platform from which it then becomes an habituated application when the relevant circumstance triggers the application.

launching center's subconscious platform: The subconscious platform is the location from which all application is made when the strategy to be applied has become habituated. A strategy becomes habituated when the same circumstance presents itself on multiple occasions and self-consciousness makes application of that strategy from the conscious platform over and over again until the strategy becomes habituated. You know when a strategy has become habituated when its application has been made without self-consciousness having to make a conscious decision to make the application.

laws of divine establishment and the four divine institutions: The laws of divine establishment and the four divine institutions are specific decrees designed by God the Father to perpetuate human history until the angelic conflict is resolved. The laws of divine establishment include every scientific law, and the four divine institutions include freedom, marriage, family, and nationalism.

phase 1, phase 2, phase 3: There are three phases of God the Father's plan for the human race: phase 1, phase 2, and phase 3.

> **phase 1:** This term applies to the salvation phase of God the Father's plan. It refers to everything God the Father decreed in eternity past to provide spiritual salvation for every unbelieving member of the human race.
>
> **phase 2:** This term applies to every principle, promise, doctrine, technique, rule for living, and operational procedure decreed by God the Father for the born-again Christian to successfully implement the Christian way of life as he or she advances from spiritual babyhood to Christian maturity.
>
> **phase 3:** This term refers to the eternal phase of God's plan for the human race. It can refer to the eternal phase of God's plan after physical death or after the Church Age believer is raptured.

paradigm: A paradigm is the totality of a human being's way of thinking based upon everything previously believed that forms the basis for interpreting everything in life; one's paradigm can contain absolute truths and distortions of absolute truth.

reference center: Reference center is a general term referring to that part of the soul's mentality that has the divinely decreed capacity to both receive and/or store data associated with the circumstances of life.

reference center[1]: Reference center[1] is the specific term used to designate that part of the soul's mentality that receives incoming data through the ear gate, eye gate, or tactilely. (Reference center[1] should be read "reference center one". Do not add the definite are "the" in front of the word reference.)

reference center[2]: Reference center[2] is the term used to designate the same reference center (general) as reference center[1]; however, the distinction is made as to whether data is being sent to the human spirit or receiving data back from the human spirit. Reference center[1] sends data to the human spirit, and reference center[2] receives data being sent back to it from the human spirit. (Reference center[2] should be read "reference center two". Do not add the definite are "the" in front of the word reference.)

self-consciousness: Self-consciousness is one of five attributes of the soul: self-consciousness, volition, mentality, emotion, and conscience.

understanding[1] (knowing[1]): This term can be somewhat confusing if thought is not given to try to remove the confusion. Understanding[1] refers to understanding something that has been said. In this sense, understanding what has been said and knowing what has been said makes understanding and knowing synonymous terms. However, neither of these two terms implies understanding or knowing the meaning of what was said. For example, if I were to ask you to repeat after me, "Tirar la casa por la ventana," your reply might be, "Man, I have no idea what you just said." In this case, my spoken words had entered your reference center[1] through your ear gate, but the end result was that you could not repeat what I said because you did not understand[1] (know) what I said. However, if I were to ask you to repeat after me, "Tirar la casa por la ventana," and you replied, "Tirar la casa por la ventana," you just demonstrated what is meant by understanding[1] (knowing[1]). You understood (knew[1]) what was said; however, if I were to ask you, "What does that mean?" you might say, "Man, I don't have any idea what that means." On the other hand, you might say, "That's a Spanish idiom that means 'to roll out the red carpet.'" The issue is this with understanding[1] (knowing[1]). You understand what was said, but without reference to whether you know the meaning of what was said maybe you do or maybe you don't – but you did understand[1] (know[1]) what was said.

understanding[2] (knowing[2]): Understanding[2] (knowing[2]) is differentiated from understanding[1] (knowing[1]) in this manner. Understanding[2] (knowing[2]) understands (knows) the meaning of what was said. Let's unconfuse the confusion – if in fact, confusion existed at all. If you were to say to someone, "Tirar la casa por la ventana," and then ask, "Do you understand what I said?" and they responded affirmatively, "Yes, I understand what you said." However, when you arrive at a designated location at 7:00 PM, the lights are out, the door is locked, and you're standing there alone. You are now wondering what happened. You were expecting a big party at 7:00 PM, but nothing was happening. So, you make a phone call, and say, "I thought you told me you understood what I had said," and the response is, "I did understand what you said." "Well, then what did I say?" "You said, "Tirar la casa por la ventana." "Well, what does that mean?" "Sir, I understand[1] (know[1]) what you said, but I have no idea what that means." There it is! There's the confusion. It's the difference between understanding[1] (knowing[1]) what was said without understanding[2] (knowing[2]) the meaning of what was said. So, when you say something to someone, and then ask that person with whom you're conversing, "Do you understand what I just said?" and they respond affirmatively, you need to make certain that the affirmative response implies understanding[2] (knowing[2]), and not just understanding[1] (knowing[1]) if you expect affirmative action associated with what you had said. Otherwise, you may be standing alone at the door at 7:00 PM, with the lights out, the door locked, and wondering what had happened between your present reality and what you thought was understood^2 (known^2).

application of understanding^1 (knowing^1) and understanding^2 (knowing^2): You are the preacher, and you are waxing eloquent, and the members of your congregation are nodding their heads affirmatively, with joyous "amens" being shouted from around the auditorium. Your heart is pounding because of the favorable response you're getting from your audience. You just know that "they're getting it." However, at a later, yet appropriate time, you discover that whatever you were preaching had no favorable response from those whom you thought had "gotten it." What happened? Well, here it is, pure and simple. The audience was nodding favorably and shouting "amens" because it understood^1 (knew^1) what you were saying, but did not understand^2 (know^2) the meaning of what you were saying. What was going on in the mind of the audience was something like this. "Man, this guy can really preach! He's something else!" And the more they nodded affirmatively and shouted their "amens," the faster your heart pounded and the louder you preached. What a let-down when you saw no favorable response to your preaching the moment it should have been being applied. You thought the congregation understood^2 (knew^2), and it did, but it was understood^1 (knew^1), not understood^2 (knew^2). "Hello!" and welcome to confusion.

want-to-want: "Want-to-want" is the positive mental attitude of a human being who has changed his mind from "I don't want the will of God for my life" to "I want-to-want the will of God for my life." The want-to-want attitude comes about when the circumstances of life have become so intolerable that this individual realizes that his don't want the will of God for his life must change. The first step out of his intolerable circumstances is to change his "I don't want the will of God for my life" to an "I want-to-want the will of God for my life." Please note that at this point nothing has changed but his attitude. His circumstances remain the same, but he has changed his attitude from "I don't want the will of God for my life" to "I want-to-want the will of God for my life."

When dealing mentally with the will of God for your life, it is possible for a human being to say, "I don't want the will of God for my life, but my circumstances are so bad that a change of attitude is necessary, and I've reached the point in my life that although I haven't wanted the will of God for my life, I now want-to-want the will of God for my life. Please learn the difference between "I want the will of God for my life" and "I want-to-want the will of God for my life." Light-years of difference exist between these two statements.

Establishing Some Concepts

Concepts of the Old-man and New-man: The concepts of old-man and new-man are found in Romans 6:6 and Colossians 3:9-10. The terminology comes from the King James Version of the Bible.

> Romans 6:6 Knowing this, that our old man is crucified with him, that the body of sin might be destroyed, that henceforth we should not serve sin. (KJV)

> Colossians 3:9 Lie not one to another, seeing that ye have put off the old man with his deeds; 10 And have put on the new man, which is renewed in knowledge after the image of him that created him: (KJV)

It may be difficult to believe, but opposition to the old-man new-man concepts has been presented to this author with the argument that if the King James Version were not the source of the terms, the old-man new-man concepts would be non-existent. Now, is that a brilliant piece of old-man logic or is that a brilliant piece of old-man logic?

Concept of the Soul: The concept of the soul is found in 432 verses in the King James Version of the Bible, but 1 Thessalonians 5:23 will be used to represent the concept.

> 1 Thessalonians 5:23 And the very God of peace sanctify you wholly; and I pray God your whole spirit and soul and body be preserved blameless unto the coming of our Lord Jesus Christ. (KJV)

Well, there it is again – that King James Version of the Bible. I pray that there aren't those out there that would say, "If you didn't use the King James Version, the soul wouldn't exit." Equally brilliant! Right?

Where It All Started

The author had been tri-hosting Sunday evening Webex meetings with Rev. Al Rosenblum, Associate Pastor of the Doctrinal Studies Church in Birmingham, Alabama, and Rev. Steven Ellis, Pastor of the Church of the Servant King in Dallas, Texas. The subject of these meetings had been the "old-man new-man concepts." During these meetings, the subject came up about reckoning the old-man dead to sin and reckoning the new-man alive unto God. It was not uncommon in these meetings to mention that that the old-man is to be reckoned dead to sin. One evening during a Monday Night Home Bible Study, a friend, Gary Johnson, raised the following question: "If the old-man is to be reckoned dead to sin, is it the new-man or the old-man that reckons the old-man dead to sin?" That question had never been asked in this author's presence prior to that time. Interestingly, however, the author had been writing a paper on the subject, *The Neutrality of the Soul,* a few weeks prior to the time that this question was asked. It was at the moment that this question was asked that the answer became clear. It is neither the old-man nor the new-man that reckons the old-man dead to sin. It's the neutral soul that reckons the old-man dead to sin. Let's explore this notion. First, does the new-man reckon the old-man dead to sin?

Does the New-man Reckon the Old-man Dead to Sin?

There are some basic assumptions that should be considered in pursuit of an answer to this question.

Basic Assumption #1: It is assumed that the soul and all of its characteristics are neutral in the sense that the soul is neither inherently sinful nor inherently spiritual; therefore, it is classified as neutral.

The human soul has five characteristics: self-consciousness, volition, mentality, emotion, and conscience. The nature of human body is sinful. The nature of the human spirit is spiritual. While the soul can be influenced by either the human body's sinful nature or the Holy Spirit who indwells the human spirit, the soul is by nature neutral because it is neither inherently sinful nor inherently spiritual.

Since the soul is neutral, its parts are neutral; therefore, self-consciousness is neutral; volition is neutral; mentality is neutral; emotion is neutral; and conscience is neutral. Remember, neutral doesn't mean "does nothing." Neutral simply implies capable of influence, but does not imply inherent sinfulness or inherent spirituality.

Self-consciousness implies awareness of self. It is the characteristic of the soul that makes a human being aware of his very existence. Philosophically, if the question were asked, "How do I know that I exist as a human being?" The answer would be that self-consciousness is the decreed characteristic of the soul that not only makes a person aware of his or her existence, it makes one aware of everything that goes on in his or her periphery. Self-consciousness is the leader of the soul, the director of the soul. Self-consciousness decides, thinks, feels, and determines the soul's standards of conscience. The soul minus self-consciousness relegates the soul to nothingness.

Volition is the characteristic of the soul that enables self-consciousness to make decisions. Volition is the characteristic that permits self-consciousness the freedom of choice. Choices are determined to be good or bad, right or wrong only when measured against the standards in the conscience of the person measuring the decision. Good and bad and right and wrong are relative terms. They are personally relative to the standards residing in a human being's conscience. If a human being holds that absolute truths exist, then a decision can be measured against the related absolute truth stored in the conscience to determine the decision's goodness, badness, rightness, or wrongness. If the existence of absolute truths is denied, then any decision being evaluated will be measured against the relative standard resident in the conscience of the person doing the evaluating. Volition does not make decisions. Self-consciousness makes all of the soul's decisions. The soul minus volition renders the soul robotic.

Mentality is the characteristic of the soul that processes data through its major centers, sub-centers, and sub-sub-centers. There are three major centers: a reference center, a memory center, and a launching center. There are two major sub-centers: a new-man clothes closet and an old-man clothes closet. Within each clothes closet there are three categories of sub-sub-centers: vocabulary, conscience, and category. The launching center also has one sub-center referred to as the growth sub-center. These sub and sub-sub centers will be listed later in this booklet to show their relationship to the three major centers. The following web link provides a PowerPoint presentation developed by Rev. Darryl Anderson that demonstrates the manner in which data is processed in and through the soul's mentality: http://www.jimbrettell.org/ppt/motns.ppt. (See Addendum #2).

Emotion is the characteristic of the soul from which feelings are generated in association with circumstances of life. Emotions can be negative or positive depending upon the standard by which they are measured. For example, hatred might be considered a negative emotion while joy might be considered a positive emotion.

Conscience is the characteristic of the soul that stores the soul's norms and standards. Norms and standards are determined when the soul's self-consciousness understands and *believes* data received into the mentality's reference center. Data stored in the conscience is data believed to be true whether the data aligns with the absolute truth of God's Word or not. For example, suppose that dancing is not really sinful; however, if a person believes that dancing is sinful, dancing will be stored in the conscience as sinful activity, and this person's conscience will be bothered if the person holding that standard makes a decision that would in some way or another violate that standard. In like manner, suppose that premarital sex is sinful; however, if a person believes that premarital sex is not sinful, premarital sex will be stored in the conscience as legitimate activity, and this person's conscience will NOT be bothered regardless of the number of occasions this person enters into the activity of premarital sexual. No, the Holy Spirit does not convict a human being of sinful activity. The Holy Spirit convicts of one sin and one sin alone, namely, the sin of unbelief (John 16:8-9). It is a person's conscience that convicts him of wrongdoing as that "wrongdoing" relates to the soul's self-consciousness using volition to make a decision that violates a norm or standard that resides in that person's conscience.

Basic Assumption #2: Faith-alone in Christ-alone and "Operation KRRY" are not synonymous. Faith-alone in Christ-alone is the divine means of becoming spiritually saved. After salvation, "Operation KRRY" is the divine means of entering the sphere of the Spirit from which sphere the believer functions in his new-man. The function of faith-alone in Christ-alone always precedes the function of "Operation KRRY."

Basic Assumption #3: If "Operation KRRY" must be implemented to enter the new-man, and "Operation KRRY" is implemented AFTER salvation, there has to be a first time for the believer to enter the new-man AFTER salvation has occurred. The issue here is one of chronology, sequence of events – first, salvation; then, "Operation KRRY."

Basic Assumption #4: Since the function of "Operation KRRY" is required to enter the new-man, and since there is a first time to enter the new-man AFTER salvation, the new-man cannot possibly be the one who reckons the old-man dead to sin. Look at the sequence:

1. Faith-alone in Christ-alone for spiritual salvation.
2. K for "knowing" that our old-man was crucified with Christ.
3. R_1 for "reckoning" the old-man dead to sin.
4. R_2 for "reckoning" the new-man alive unto God.
5. Y for "yielding to God the Holy Spirit.
6. Immediate entrance into the sphere of the Spirit and function from the source of the new-man.

Basic Assumption #5: Since the concept of "Operation KRRY" is consistent with absolute truth, and the absolute truth regarding "Operation KRRY" must be internalized (understood^2 and believed^2) before functioning in "Operation KRRY" the principle is that you cannot do what you do not know and the function of "Operation

KRRY" is the means of entering the new-man, then reckoning the old-man dead to sin cannot be a work of the new-man.

Conclusion: Following the line of thinking presented in the five basic assumptions, it cannot be the new-man that reckons the old-man dead to sin.

Does the Old–Man Reckon the Old-Man Dead to Sin?

<u>Question:</u> If Satan's kingdom cannot stand if Satan casts out Satan, why should you believe that the old-man is reckoned dead to sin by the old-man reckoning himself dead to sin?

> Matthew 12:26 And if Satan cast out Satan, he is divided against himself; how shall then his kingdom stand? (KJV)

If further evidence is needed, consider the following:

1. The six sequential steps above represent both logical and chronological order.
2. If the old-man is reckoned dead (R_1) at step 3, and the new-man is not accessed until step 6, it is impossible for the old-man to have reckoned the old-man dead to sin because the old-man is reckoned dead to sin at step 3 and the new-man is not entered until step 6.

Conclusion: It cannot be the old-man that reckons the old-man dead to sin.

The Old-Man Is Reckoned Dead by the Neutral Soul

<u>**Thesis:**</u> It is the neutral soul, specifically the neutral self-consciousness, that reckons the old-man dead to sin, and the remainder of this booklet is dedicated to the support of this thesis.

Yes, there are thirty-three pages that follow, however, the volume of information that follows not only supports the thesis, but places in writing the thoughts that were generated in the author's mind as he contemplated the thesis. He believes that every piece of information that follows is important to our complete new-man belief system. Truth withstands the most careful scrutiny. In the interest of arriving at the deepest truths possible in support of our Christian life, the author is open to any and all comments regarding any facet of information contained in this booklet.

This booklet is provided to challenge your thinking and to equip you with a deeper understanding of how your Christian life is designed to function, presupposing that this booklet contains absolute truth.

Introductory Information That Builds a Solid Foundation

Regarding this entire booklet, a very legitimate question might be asked. If the information that follows is correct, then why does it work this way? The answer is simply because it was decreed by God the Father to work this way.

What follows is some introductory information that builds a solid foundation for Christian thinking.

1. The born-again Christian is a trichotomous being (1 Thessalonians 5:23):

   - spirit.
   - soul.
   - body.

2. The nature of the trichotomous being:

   - the body is the residence of the sin nature; therefore, the body is sinful in nature.
   - the soul is neutral, but receives influence from the sin nature and Holy Spirit.

- the spirit is the residence of the Holy Spirit; therefore, it is spiritual in nature.

3. The soul has five characteristics:

    - self-consciousness.
    - volition.
    - mentality.
    - emotion.
    - conscience.

4. The mentality of the soul can be categorized in two ways:

    A. First Way:

    - the conscious mind.
        - embraces both (nous) and (kardia).
    - the subconscious mind.

    B. Second Way:

    - reference center (nous).
    - spiritual heart (kardia).

5. There are three major centers (1, 2, 3), three sub-centers (A, B, C), and six sub-sub-centers (1, 2, 3, 4, 5, 6) in the soul's conscious mind. Consider the following major centers, sub-centers, and sub-sub-centers:

   (nous).
      1) Reference Center.
   (kardia).
        2. Memory Center.
           A. New-man clothes closet.
              1) Vocabulary Center.
              2) Category Center.
              3) Conscience Center.
           B. Old-man clothes closet

                4) Vocabulary Center.
                5) Category Center.
                6) Conscience Center.
        3. Launching Center.
            C. Growth Center.

6. Data received into the both the new-man and old-man clothes closet is stored in centers referred to as vocabulary, categories, and conscience.

    - new-man clothing is stored in the new-man clothes closet as absolute truth.
    - absolute truth stored as new-man vocabulary
    - absolute truth stored as new-man categories
    - absolute truth stored as new-man conscience
    - old-man clothing is stored in the old-man clothes closet as distortions of absolute truth.
    - distorted truth stored as old-man vocabulary
    - distorted truth stored as old-man categories
    - distorted truth stored as old-man conscience

7. R.B. Thieme, Jr., identifies four divine institutions in his tape series, *Spiritual Dynamics 784, 789, 2/8/96*. This author amplifies the concept of nationalism:

    - freedom.
    - marriage.
    - family.
    - nationalism.
        ➤ capitalism.
        ➤ free-market economy.

8. Data received through the ear gate, eye gate, or tactilely as incoming at reference center[1] can be categorized in two ways:

    - absolute truth: a decree of God the Father as He determines the decree to be understood.

- distorted truth (evil): any distortion of a divine decree no matter how slight the distortion.

9. Evil (distortions of truth) can be categorized in two ways:

    - **evil principle:** the distortion of any absolute truth that has been decreed by God the Father.
    - **evil practice:** the practice (application) of any evil principle to a life situation.

    Examples of an evil principle and an evil practice:

    evil principle: Tithing was giving Israel under the Mosaic Law. Giving any amount as led by the Holy Spirit is Christian giving. To state that the Christian is to tithe his income is a distortion of truth and falls into the category of being an "evil principle."

    evil practice: If a Christian accepts the evil principle that tithing is Christian giving, and then practices tithing, the Christian has involved himself in an evil practice.

10. There are three categories of people who actualize (apply) internalized data from the soul's launching center:

    A. Who actualizes (applies) data from the launching center?

        - natural man (1 Corinthians 2:14): an unbeliever functioning from the source of the old-man.
        - carnal man (1 Corinthians 3:1): a believer functioning from the source of the old-man.
        - spiritual man (1 Corinthians 2:15): a believer functioning from the source of the new-man.

    B. Who internalizes data? Any human being using the neutral self-consciousness and volition can internalize data.

11. There are two categories of function when actualizing (applying) data from the launching center:

    - old-man function.
    - new-man function.

12. Truths found in the Word of God can be categorized in the following manners:

    A. One Way:

    1) historical narrative.
    2) hortatory truth (biblical commands).
    3) spiritual truth.

    B. Another Way:

    1) laws of divine establishment and the four divine institutions.
    2) Gospel.
    3) royal family honor code.

13. The Holy Spirit's ministry to a believer during the times of internalization and actualization are *active* and *passive*:

    internalization: the Holy Spirit actively teaches, confirms, and witnesses to the human spirit.
    actualization: the Holy Spirit passively infuses the believer when the believer yields to God the Holy Spirit in the fourth step of "Operation KRRY."

More Foundational Information

The following information assumes that the believer has confessed personal sin(s) according to 1 John 1:9. It is not essential for you to determine whether the believer is functioning from the old-man or the new-man because neither is a factor in the process of internalizing data from the printed pages of the Word of God to the launching center of one's soul. Neither the old-man nor the new-man are factors when processing data that is either read or heard audibly.

1. The Word of God starts out as data (information) on the printed pages of the Bible.

2. The believer's self-consciousness becomes aware of data being internalized at reference center[1] in the following manners:

   - Data is internalized through the ear gate by the sighted, the hearing, and the blind.
   - Data is internalized through the eye gate by the sighted, hearing, and deaf.
   - Data is internalized tactilely by those who are both deaf and blind.

3. The following possibilities prevail when the process of internalizing data is underway:

   - The believer processes data without having confessed or wanting-to-want the will of God for his life.
   - The believer processes data after confessing, but without wanting-to-want the will of God for his life.
   - The believer processes data after confessing and wanting-to-want the will of God for his life.

4. When the believer is processing data at reference center[1]:

   - Reference center[1] is the initial center of the soul's mentality to encounter incoming data.
   - The data received as incoming at reference center[1], but not understood[1], is rejected for residence in reference center[1].
   - The data received as incoming at reference center[1], and understood[1], is accepted for residence in reference center[1].
   - The data received as incoming at reference center[1] can be both understood[1] and believed[1].
   - The data believed[1] may be truth.
   - The data believed[1] may be distorted truth (evil principle).

- The data believed[1] when incoming at reference center[1] is stored in reference center[1] and processed to the next center.
- It can be processed to the memory center, or . . .
- It can be processed to the human spirit.

5. What is the basis upon which incoming *absolute truth* is received into reference center[1], but remains in reference center[1], and *cannot* be processed any further at the time it is received into reference center[1]?

    - The basis upon which incoming *absolute truth* remains in reference center[1] and cannot be processed any further at the time it is received into reference center[1] is twofold:
        - The believer has unconfessed sin in his or her life and is therefore unclean before the Lord.
        - The believer is clean before the Lord, but has no desire to want-to-want *absolute truth*.
    - This *absolute truth* will remain in reference center[1] and be the basis upon which the believer will be able to say that he or she has a frame of reference for this piece of *absolute truth*, but it will be of no spiritual value until it is processed through the human spirit, and that cannot be accomplished until the believer is clean before the Lord and wanting-to-want the *absolute truth*.
    - Until *absolute truth* is processed through the human spirit, the believer has NO confirmation from the Holy Spirit that this *absolute truth* received is in fact *absolute truth*. It is treated as academic information about which the believer can say that he or she has a frame of reference – "sure, I've heard of that" – but it will be of no spiritual value until it has been confirmed in the human spirit by the Holy Spirit.

6. What is the basis upon which incoming *absolute truth* is processed from reference center[1] to the human spirit?

    - The basis upon which incoming *absolute truth* is processed from reference center[1] to the human spirit is the fact that the believer is clean before the Lord through confession of all post-salvation sin and wanting-to-want absolute truth.

7. What is the basis upon which incoming *distorted truth* is processed from reference center[1] to the human spirit?

   - There is NO basis upon which distorted truth enters the human spirit. Distorted truth NEVER reaches the human spirit; therefore, distorted truth is NEVER confirmed as distorted by the Holy Spirit.

8. How is incoming *distorted truth* processed by the believer who is unclean before the Lord and/or does not want-to-want absolute truth.

   - If distorted truth entering reference center[1] is NOT understood[1], it is rejected by self-consciousness and will NOT be stored in reference center[1].
   - If distorted truth entering reference center[1] is understood[1] and believed[1] by self-consciousness, it is stored in reference center[1] as a frame of reference and is immediately processed as old-man clothing to the launching center. This data does not go into the old-man clothes closet at this time. It goes from reference center[1] directly to the launching center.
   - This data by-passes the old-man clothes closet at this time and does not go to the old-man clothes closet until self-consciousness takes it off the launching center's subconscious platform, placing it in the old-man clothes closet while simultaneously moving the pertinent piece of new-man clothing from the new-man clothes closet to the conscious platform of the launching center.

9. There are two ways in which self-consciousness recognizes data coming into reference center[1] as *distorted truth*:

   - The believer has the pertinent *absolute truth* stored as a frame of reference in reference center[1] by which to measure the incoming data and recognizes the incoming data as distorted because it does not match or fit the believer's present paradigm. Under this condition, namely, that this believer has a frame of reference for the incoming data, it makes no difference whether the believer is functioning from the old-man or the new-man or whether he or she is clean before the Lord or wanting-to-want absolute truth. The issue here is that the believer has a frame of reference against which self-consciousness can measure incoming data.

- The believer is clean before the Lord and wanting-to-want *absolute truth*, but receives no confirmation from the Holy Spirit within the human spirit that the incoming data is *absolute truth*. Therefore, by default, the incoming data is recognized as distorted because there is no Holy Spirit confirmation. This implies that this believer has learned or is learning to recognize the Holy Spirit's ministry within his own human spirit.

10. What happens to data coming into reference center[1] as *distorted truth* but is not understood[1] by the soul's neutral self-consciousness?

- Data coming into reference center[1] as *distorted truth*, but not understood[1] by the neutral self-consciousness, is rejected by the neutral self-consciousness for storage in reference center[1].
- By divine decree, reference center[1] will not and cannot store what the neutral self-consciousness doesn't understand.
- The fact that reference center[1] cannot and will not store what the neutral self-consciousness doesn't understand implies that the neutral self-consciousness has no future frame of reference for that particular distorted truth that has been rejected because it wasn't understood.

What Is Meant by Wanting-to-Want

Philippians 2:13 For it is God which worketh in you both to will and to do of his good pleasure. (KJV)

1. Please note that if God IS working in the born-again Christian to will His good pleasure, the implication is that this believer does NOT will God's good pleasure for himself at the time God is working in him; otherwise, there would be no good reason for God to be working in this believer to accomplish what was already true of the believer's life.

   A. This believer might be saying it this way: "I do not will God's good pleasure for myself."

   B. In today's language, this believer is saying, "I'm not interested in God's plan for my life."

   C. When it's understood that from the moment a person is saved, he continues to function under the old-man belief system, it's easy to understand why this born-again Christian would not want God's good pleasure for himself. It's the very nature of the old-man to NOT want God's good pleasure for himself.

2. This verse also discloses a second problem in the believer's life.

   A. Because this believer doesn't want God's good pleasure for himself, he will not DO what God wants him to DO.

   B. Look at it:

      1) He will not DO God's good pleasure, because . . .
      2) He doesn't WANT God's good pleasure.

3. Understand the following: Man was placed on this planet by God the Father to resolve the angelic conflict through obedience to the Father's will for his life during the respective dispensation in which he lives. Yet, as a born-again Christian he begins his Christian life unwilling to DO the will of God for his life. Why? It's because he doesn't WANT the will of God for his life. Therefore, it isn't difficult to understand why God the Father through His omniscience in eternity past was able to decree the circumstances for this believer's life to get his attention to

change his want-to. Until now, the believer not only didn't want God's good pleasure, he didn't even want-to-want God's good pleasure for his life. To this Christian we can say, "Sir, say 'hello' to the circumstances of your life."

4. The circumstances of a believer's life are divinely designed for one of two purposes: divine discipline or divine testing.

   1) Divine discipline: This is God the Father using adverse circumstances to get your attention because you are outside of His will for your life.

   2) Divine testing: This is God the Father using adverse circumstances to stretch your faith for the purpose of your personal spiritual growth.

The Believer and God the Father's Will

1. After becoming born-again, when the new believer finally hears the truth concerning God the Father's will for "phase 2" of his Christian life, the following options are available to the believer:

   - the new believer can continue to reject His will.
   - at first he rejected God's will through ignorance of what that will is.
   - later, after learning God's will for his life, he chooses to reject God's will knowing precisely what that will is.
   - the new believer delays the pursuit of God's will.
   - the new believer begins the pursuit of God's will.

2. If the believer chooses to reject or delay the pursuit of the Father's will, the believer's circumstances are divinely designed to capture his attention to enlighten him that he has a destiny related to the resolution of the angelic conflict.

   A. The question arises as to how long it will take, if ever in temporal life, for the new believer to personally acknowledge the destiny that God the Father has designed for him.

B. <u>Major point that must be understood:</u> The Holy Spirit can offer this believer NO help until he acknowledges that his circumstances of life are directing him to change his attitude toward the will of God for his life. His attitude: "I don't want the will of God for my life, and that's only the half of it. The other half is that I don't even want to change my mind about not wanting the will of God for my life."

   1) Consider this statement: "I don't want-to-want" the will of God for my life.

      - There are two "want to's" in this statement.
      - Note the seriousness of the following statement:
      - "I don't want-to-want God's destiny for my life."
      - Your comment: "Well, sir, you should change your 'I don't want-to-want God's destiny for my life' to 'I want-to-want God's destiny for my life.'"
      - His response: "I don't want God's destiny for my life, and I don't want to change my mind about not wanting God's destiny for my life."
      - If only one "don't-want-to" existed, the door would be open to a change of mind, but by saying "I don't-want-to-want" the will of God for my life, this firmly rejects God's destiny for his life, unless of course, a change of thinking occurs later.

   2) Please, contemplate the seriousness of this "don't-want-to-want" scenario. This is tantamount to the "hardened heart" spoken of in the King James Version.

      Mark 6:52 For they [unbelievers] considered not the miracle of the loaves: for their *heart was hardened.* (KJV)

      Ephesians 4:19 *Who being past feeling* [this refers to a believer's hardened heart] have given themselves over unto lasciviousness, to work all uncleanness with greediness. (KJV)

C. When the new believer finally "caves-in" because of the pressure of his circumstances, and acknowledges that God is seeking his attention, and begins to want-to-want the truth of God's will for his life, the following can begin to occur:

1) Absolute truth can now begin to be moved from reference center[1] into the human spirit.

2) The Holy Spirit can now begin to do the following:

   a. The Holy Spirit can *confirm* as absolute the absolute truths already in the believer's reference center[1]. (Note: To *confirm* is only `"what" the Holy Spirit can do; this is not "how" He will do it. The "how" will be discussed later.)

   b. The Holy Spirit can *confirm* as absolute any absolute truth now being conveyed to the believer whether it is being conveyed to him through the ear gate, eye gate, or tactilely.

      1 The believer will not hear voices or have a vision that confirms absolute truth to be absolute truth.

      2 The believer will recognize the truth as absolute simply by "knowing that he knows that he knows" that he has received confirmation in his human spirit from the Holy Spirit.

   c. HOW does this work? The Holy Spirit resides in the human spirit. The human spirit is designed by God the Father to be a receptor organ to *receive* and *transmit* communication from the Holy Spirit to the believer who has met the conditions to receive this communication. The conditions for receiving transmitted communication from the Hoy Spirit is that the believer must be clean before the Lord through confession of post-salvation sins and he must "want-to-want" the will of God for his life. When the Holy Spirit speaks, He speaks with an inaudible voice that addresses the human spirit. By divine decree, the human spirit receives this communication and then transmits it. By divine decree, reference center^2 of the soul's mentality receives this transmission from the human spirit and interprets what the Spirit is saying. The missing link, if it can be called the missing link, has been the believer "wanting-to-want" the will of God for his life after having confessed known sins. From a believer's condition of being clean before the Lord through up-to-date confession of post-salvation sins and "wanting-to-want" the will of God for his life, the Holy Spirit can begin His communicative ministry in the human spirit, but not one second prior to the believer's "wanting-to-want" preceded by confession!

4. Note the following truths contained in Philippians 2:13:

    Philippians 2:13 For it is God which worketh in you both to will and to do of his good pleasure. (KJV)

    A. The believer doesn't want the will of God for his life.

    B. Because the believer doesn't want the will of God for his life, he doesn't want to DO the will of God for his life.

5. Note that God the Father is at work in the believer's life to accomplish two things:

    - He wants to change the believer's will from "I don't want-to-want" to "I want-to-want."
    - He wants to change what the believer thinks because the believer has been thinking "I don't-want-to-want" the will of God for my life.

6. From the outset of salvation, little to nothing has changed in the believer's life except his spiritual status from being lost to now being saved.

7. The new believer MAY HAVE the following data available in his reference center[1] and perhaps even on the launching center of the soul at the moment of salvation:

   A. Some absolute truths regarding the laws of divine establishment and the four divine institutions.

   B. Just enough absolute truth regarding the gospel to have become saved.

   C. Some doctrinal information associated with the gospel regarding how-to become saved.

   D. A reference center[1] full of doctrinal information about which the believer is able to say to you, "Yeah, sure, I've heard about that." This means that he has a frame of reference for something about which he is now hearing. What might have been the source of his frame of reference? Well, he might have heard it from his parents or perhaps heard it from others. Did he understand[1] what he had heard? Yes. Did he perhaps even believe[1] these things prior to salvation? Yes, but he only believed[1] academically. They had not yet been confirmed by the Holy Spirit from within the human spirit. He is able to recall these truths and even be somewhat conversant on the subject.

8. The issue is that even though salvation has taken place, there may be no will (want-to-want) to fulfill the destiny that God has for every believer.

   For the new believer to have no will (no want-to-want) to go beyond salvation is not uncommon, and even quite natural because the new believer may not have any information stored in his reference center[1] that indicates a knowledge[1] of, an understanding[1] of, or a belief[1] in the decreed destiny of every born-again Church Age believer, namely, to become exactly like Jesus Christ in His humanity.

9. This is where both God the Father and the Holy Spirit work together to change the believer's will (his not-wanting-to-want).

   A. Prior to this time, concerning God the Father's will for the believer's life, if you were to say to the believer, "Do you want the will of God for your life?" the believer might respond in this manner. "I don't want the Father's will for my life. I am totally satisfied with my eternal salvation."

   B. You might further respond: "Do you want-to-want the Father's will for your life?" You may hear one of two things:

      1) "I don't-want-to-want the will of God for my life."

      2) "Even though I don't want the will of God for my life, I want-to-want the will of God for my life."

   C. The difference between these two statements, B.1) and B.2), is the difference between loss of escrow blessing-in-time and loss of escrow reward-in-eternity or the distribution of escrow blessing-in-time and the distribution of escrow reward-in-eternity.

   D. It's because of the believer's "don't-want-to-want" that God the Father initiates His decreed plan to provide circumstances designed to bring this believer to see the destiny He has decreed for his life.

   E. God the Father has decreed circumstance after circumstance designed to bring about a "want-to-want" in the believer's life.

   F. Until now, the believer's "want-to-want" is "I don't-want-to-want."

G. Even though the believer may not want-to-want the will of God, through God the Father's ordering of circumstances, the believer's "don't-want-to-want the will of God" can change from "I don't-want-to-want" to an "I want-to-want" God's will for my life.

H. Please note this! "I didn't want-to-want, but NOW, I-want-to-want." It's the second "want" that's important to our understanding. It's this second "want" that is in focus in Philippians 2:13.

I. While the believer is dealing with his circumstances decreed by God the Father, failure after failure may occur.

   1) This means that the believer is failing to avail himself of God the Father's grace provision (new-man strategy/solution) to deal with his circumstances.

   2) The believer generally believes that the solution to the circumstances of his life lies within himself, or perhaps with some other human being who can deliver him.

   3) It's possible that through his circumstances this believer will reach a point of "wanting-to-want" the will of God for his life. This occurs when he realizes that since none of his solutions have worked, there must be better way, and he turns to God the Father and His solutions.

J. Now, it's the Holy Spirit's turn.

   1) When the believer's "want-to-want" is brought about by his life's circumstances, assuming that he is confessed-up-to-date, the Holy Spirit can now begin to confirm as absolute truth those absolute truths stored in the believer's reference center[1], heretofore, unconfirmed.

   2) Functioning under the principles of confession and "wanting-to-want," if a circumstance triggers the recall of a piece of data that resides in reference center[1], the

principle of "wanting-to-want" further triggers that data to be transferred from reference center[1] to the human spirit where the Holy Spirit responds in the human spirit with a confirming "Beloved, that's absolute truth." No, you didn't hear a voice. You just know that you know that you know that data has just been confirmed as truth by the Holy Spirit in your human spirit.

3) When circumstances of life trigger other information contained in reference center[1], and perhaps even in the memory center, the "want-to-want" principle causes this data to be transferred to the human spirit to be dealt with by the Holy Spirit. Here, the Holy Spirit continues, "Yep, that's absolute truth, also." No, you are still not hearing a voice. You just know that you know that you know!

4) The key to activating Holy Spirit ministry in the believer's human spirit is the believer's "wanting-to-want" the will of God for his or her life preceded by confession, if confession was necessary.

5) "Wanting-to-want" is tantamount to saying to God the Father, "I am ready. I am sick-and-tired-of-being-sick-and-tired of having no inner happiness that comes from You."

6) Here's a principle of life: Man's extremity becomes God's opportunity. Another way of saying it is to say, "The way up is down." When you finally come to the end of your own failed solutions, God the Holy Spirit can become involved – if you allow Him to become involved. When you finally hit "the bottom" in your life, the only way remaining is "up" into Christ-likeness.

7) The principle amplified: Man's extremity brought on by the circumstances of life that were decreed by God the Father becomes the Holy Spirit's opportunity to begin to confirm absolute truth to the believer.

8) Data believed[1] at the incoming reference center[1] cannot be confirmed as absolute truth until it is confirmed by the Holy Spirit's witness in the believer's human spirit.

   a. Without confirmation, the believer may think that what he has received is absolute truth, but it's NOT.

   b. Without confirmation, the believer may think that what he has received is absolute truth, and it IS.

      <u>1</u> The issue is whether the Holy Spirit has confirmed or not confirmed.

      <u>2</u> The Holy Spirit's teaching ministry is one of confirmation in the human spirit of what was first received into reference center[1] through the ear gate, eye gate, or tactilely.

         <u>a</u> The confirming ministry of the Holy Spirit is why human I.Q. is not the final issue, but human I.Q. is a factor in being able to understand[1] more complex issues received at reference center[1].

         <u>b</u> Believers with a lower I.Q. do well with concrete data, but begin to lose ability to understand[1] when abstract thought is required (this last thought is not meant to be demeaning; it's objective reality).

The Holy Spirit's Role in This Process

1. The Holy Spirit takes up residence and permanently resides in the born-again Christian's human spirit from the moment that salvation occurs.

2. Two of the Holy Spirit's ministries within the human spirit are as follows:

- The Holy Spirit *teaches* the believer's human spirit.
- The Holy Spirit *bears witness with* (confirms within) the believer's human spirit.

3. A distinction should be made between the roles of the Holy Spirit when absolute truth is being internalized and when it is being actualized (applied).

   A. The Holy Spirit has an *active* role when absolute truth is being internalized.

   B. The Holy Spirit has a *passive* role when absolute truth is being actualized (applied).

4. The prerequisites by which a believer accesses the ministries of the Holy Spirit are twofold.

   A. For His *active* ministry associated with internalization, rebound and "wanting-to-want" are required.

   B. For His *passive* ministry associated with actualization, yieldedness as the fourth step in "Operation KRRY" is required.

5. Major point for consideration: When the Holy Spirit is functioning in His teaching ministry within the human spirit, it is always in conjunction with data previously received through the ear gate, eye gate, or tactilely at the incoming reference center[1]. The Holy Spirit isn't just grabbing new ideas out of the air and passing them along to the believer. He works on data having already been received in the incoming reference center[1]. His work in the human spirit is teaching and witnessing (confirmation), not revelation. While referred to as His work, His ministries are His works. *Illumination* takes place in the human mind's reference center[2]. The Holy Spirit doesn't work directly ON the mind. He works directly IN the human spirit. The human mind's reference center[2] functions as a receiver that receives communication transmitted to it from the human spirit. The Holy

Spirit teaches and witnesses (confirms). The human spirit receives and transmits; and then the human mind's reference center^2 receives what the human spirit has transmitted to it. The soul's self-consciousness then functions to make spiritual sense out of what reference center^2 has received from the Holy Spirit via the human spirit. Illumination is the soul's self-consciousness experiencing an "ah-ha!" moment.

When the Holy Spirit is doing His teaching, confirming, bearing witness with our human spirit, these ministries are WHAT He does, without telling us HOW He does it. It is when we do not have a clear understanding of the mechanics of the HOW that misinterpretations of scripture creep into our theology, disrupting spiritual lives to the point of destroying personal impact in the resolution of the angelic conflict. The HOW of the Holy Spirit's teaching, confirming, bearing witness ministries needs to be explored and eventually understood[2].

6. The Holy Spirit's role in teaching, confirming, and bearing witness is *active*, not passive. He is *actually* teaching, confirming, and bearing witness. This says WHAT He does, but does not say HOW He does it.

7. The question arises regarding the believer's spiritual status that enables him or her to recognize that the source of the teaching, confirming, and bearing witness is coming from the Holy Spirit as opposed to something he or she has "figured-out" for himself or herself and then attributed to the Holy Spirit.

8. Who then reckons the old-man dead indeed to the sin nature?

    - Is it the old-man that reckons the old-man dead to the sin nature?
    - Is it the new-man that reckons the old-man dead to the sin nature?

9. The answer to the question is that it's neither the old-man nor the new-man. It's the soul's neutral self-consciousness that reckons the old-man dead to sin, and here's how this works.

A. The soul that reckons the old-man dead to sin is neutral.

B. The soul's characteristics are as follows:

- self-consciousness.
- volition.
- mentality.
- emotion.
- conscience.

10. Consider self-consciousness:

    A. Self-consciousness makes the soul aware of its own existence (the soul is the real you).

    B. Self-consciousness is the soul's leader and is inter-related with mentality, emotion, and conscience.

    - Self consciousness thinks because it is inter-related with mentality.
    - Self-consciousness emotes (feels) because it is inter-related with emotion.
    - Self-consciousness is convinced of right doing or wrong doing because it is inter-related with conscience.

    C. It is self-consciousness that makes all of the soul's decisions (choices).

    D. The degree to which the self-consciousness is aware of self determines the degree to which mentality, volition, emotion, and the conscience can function.

11. Consider volition:

    A. Volition is the decreed capacity for decision making.

    B. Volition should not be viewed as a phenomenon separate and unrelated with self-consciousness.

1) Volition and self-consciousness are united with one another. They operate together as a unit.

   2) Capacity to decide is unique to self-consciousness.

C. Mentality decides nothing; mentality is the storage center that contains data upon which self-consciousness makes decisions.

D. Emotion decides nothing; emotion provides a measure of both positive and negative feelings experienced by self-consciousness.

E. Conscience decides nothing; conscience stores data that forms the norms and standards by which self-consciousness determines the rightness or wrongness of its decision making.

12. Self-consciousness continued:

A. If the neutral self-consciousness has reached the point of "wanting-to want" regarding a pursuit of God the Father's decreed plan for itself, the following will occur:

   1) As the neutral self-consciousness becomes aware of data coming into the mentality's reference center[1] through the ear gate, eye gate, or tactilely, because it "wants to want" the will of God, it is open to the Holy Spirit's teaching, confirming, witnessing ministry that occurs in the human spirit.

       a. The Holy Spirit can only confirm in the human spirit the content that self-consciousness understands[1] after it is received into reference center[1].

           (1) Caution here: In the past, we have used the word "understand" to mean the "ah-ha" moment that occurred when the human mind understood what

the Spirit was "teaching" the human spirit. Please go back to our definitions. We need to distinguish the word "understand" in two different ways:

(a) First, <u>understanding the **content** of what is heard or read:</u> When information comes into reference center[1] through the ear gate, eye gate, or tactilely, if the **content** of what is being received is not clearly understood[1], it will be rejected as not understandable, and will never reach the Holy Spirit in the human spirit.

> For example, if your primary language is English, and you speak no other language, and you visit a Russian Orthodox church, and the entire service is conducted in Russian, don't expect the Holy Spirit to teach you anything if you understood[1] nothing of what was said.

> For example, if your pastor is using theological terms about which you have no understanding[1], do not expect the Holy Spirit to confirm the **content** of any part of his message that you did not understand[1].

(b) <u>Understanding the **meaning** of the content:</u> When incoming data is understood[1] in reference center[1] and is processed into the human spirit, when the Holy Spirit teaches, witnesses, confirms that data as absolute truth and the human spirit transmits it back to reference center[2], the moment self-consciousness has its "ah-ha" moment concerning what the Spirit has taught, witnessed, or confirmed, now, the understanding^2 is one of ***meaning*** as opposed to understanding^1 ***content***.

(2) The Holy Spirit cannot and will not teach, witness, or confirm any information not understood^1 when it first enters reference center^1.

- Confirmation is one manner in which the Holy Spirit teaches.
- His teaching ministry is one of confirming in the human spirit what self-consciousness first understood^1 at the incoming reference center^1.

(a) The Holy Spirit cannot work with data that is understood^2 only by the communicator. What is communicated must be equally understood^1 by the recipient at the recipient's incoming reference center^1.

(b) Communicators who constantly teach at their own highest level of understanding^2 rarely see an "ah-ha" moment in their target audience.

(c) Communicators must learn to teach on the level of understanding^1 of their target audience.

(d) Communicator's fail in ministry when their goal is to teach a set of notes rather than teaching people. This failure is manifested when a communicator believes that a certain point should be reached in a set of notes by the end of a teaching time period.

(e) Authors must also have in mind a target audience and realize that those outside the target audience are not likely to receive Holy Spirit confirmation of what he or she writes.

> Therefore, it is important for an author to know his or her target audience.

B. Assume for a moment that a believer is operating under the principles of rebound and "wanting-to-want" the will of God for his life. When the concepts of know, reckon, reckon, yield, and do the truth are taught, and the believer's neutral self-consciousness understands[1] this information, the Holy Spirit is then able to teach, witness, confirm this information in the human spirit, and an "ah-ha" can occur in reference center[2]. When the "ah-ha" moment occurs, self-consciousness must then decide (use it's volitional capacity) to determine whether to believe[2] or not.

If the information is believed[2], it is processed immediately through the memory center into the new-man vocabulary center, the new-man category center, and the new-man conscience center. It does not go to the growth center or the launching center until self-consciousness decides (makes a volitional decision) to remove an evil principle (old-man clothing) from the launching center and replace it with the relevant absolute truth (new-man clothing) present in the new-man clothes closet.

C. This is the manner in which every principle, promise, doctrine, technique, rule for living, and operational procedure is received into the incoming reference center[1] and processed all the way to the launching center.

Who Reckons the Old-man Dead to Sin?

The question might be asked once again. Who reckons the old-man dead indeed unto sin? Is it the old-man or the new-man? The answer: Neither. It's the soul's neutral self-consciousness that reckons the old-man dead to sin.

Let's take a look at the very first occasion that the old-man is reckoned dead to sin:

Step #1:

- Assume that the data coming into reference center[1] is Romans 6:6.
- The neutral self-consciousness is aware of this incoming data, the content of which is understood[1].
- If the neutral self-consciousness is operating under the principles of rebound and "wanting-to-want," the incoming data is processed to the human spirit.
- The Holy Spirit confirms the data as absolute truth.
- The confirmed truth is transmitted back to reference center[2] where the neutral self-consciousness has an "ah-ha" moment.
- The neutral self-consciousness then believes[2] (trusts, accepts) the truth that God the Father says that his old-man was crucified with Christ.
- Reference center[2] stores this data in reference center[2].
- Reference center[2] then copies this data and processes it to the memory center's new-man clothes closet's three sub-sub-centers: the vocabulary center, the category center, and the conscience center.
- The principle of "knowing that the old-man was crucified with Christ" goes no further at this time. It remains in the new-man clothes-closet.
- This first step of "knowing" is now complete and MUST precede "reckoning the old-man dead to sin."

Step #2

- Assume that the data coming into reference center[1] is now Romans 6:11.
- The neutral self-consciousness is aware of this incoming data, the content of which is understood[1].
- Because the neutral self-consciousness is operating under the principles of rebound and "wanting-to-want," the incoming data is processed to the human spirit.
- The Holy Spirit confirms the data as absolute truth.

- The confirmed truth is transmitted back to reference center^2 where the neutral self-consciousness has an "ah-ha" moment.
- The neutral self-consciousness then believes^2 (trusts, accepts) the truth that it must "reckon the old-man dead to sin."
- Reference center^2 stores this data in reference center^2.
- Reference center^2 then copies this data and processes it to the memory center's new-man clothes closet's three sub-sub-centers: the vocabulary center, the category center, and the conscience center.
- This second step, "reckoning the old-man dead to sin," is now complete and must precede "reckoning the new-man alive unto God."

The old-man has just been experientially reckoned dead to sin by the soul's neutral self-consciousness separate and apart from either old-man or new-man function. Neither the old-man nor the new-man has any part in reckoning the old-man dead to sin. It was accomplished solely by the soul's neutral self-consciousness.

Until now, the born-again Christian has yet to experience new-man function because the four step process leading to new-man function has been carried out only through the first two steps.

Step #3: Step #3, "reckoning the new-man alive", is carried out in precisely the same manner as steps 1 and 2.

Step #4: Step #4, "yielding to God the Holy Spirit", is carried out in precisely the same manner as steps 1, 2, and 3.

- When Step #4 has been completed, the born-again Christian is now said to be operating "in the sphere of the Spirit" from which sphere actualization (application) of new-man clothing can be made to a life situation; however, old-man clothing must be removed from the launching center one piece at a time and the pertinent piece of new-man clothing transferred from the new-man clothes closet to the launching center before it can be applied. Operating in the sphere of the spirit does not imply that every piece of new-man clothing is located at the launching center. It means only that when the believer is functioning in the sphere of the Spirit, he is functioning in the sphere of the Spirit. The believer can only apply whatever new-man clothing is located at the launching center at the moment new-man application is required. If old-man clothing remains resident at the launching center's subconscious platform, and a life situation triggers an old-man habituated reaction, the believer simultaneously reverts to old-man function because the old-man is tied to every piece of old-man clothing resident at the launching center. This is the "curse" associated with the believer who has not yet reached spiritual maturity.

One More Time

1. The Holy Spirit's role during the process of *internalization* is one of teaching, confirming, and bearing witness.

   - This is an ACTIVE role.
   - It is accomplished in the human spirit.
   - It requires incoming data that is understood[1] in reference center[1].
   - It requires the believer to be operating in rebound and "wanting-to-want" the will of God for his life.

2. The Holy Spirit's role during the process of *actualization* is characterized as follows:

   - This is a PASSIVE role.
   - The Holy Spirit passively infuses the believer.
   - The believer passively absorbs the Holy Spirit.
   - The organic connection between the believer and the Spirit results in the production of Christ's character emanating from the life of the born-again Christian from which lifestyle the impact of Christian service is maximized.
   - The organic connection between the believer and the Spirit results in the appropriation of blessing-in-time and reward-in-eternity.

ADDENDUM #1

Just a Bit of Reasoning: There are four steps in "Operation KRRY" followed by a result:

Step 1: know
Step 2: reckon^1
Step 3: reckon^2
Step 4: yield
Result: enter the sphere of the Spirit activating new-man function.

Now, A Bit of Logic

If a numbering system is 1, 2, 3, 4, 5 where 1 precedes 2, and 2 precedes 3, and 3 precedes 4, and 4 precedes 5, then 2 must precede 5.

If each number is associated with an event, it is impossible for the event at step 5 to precede step 2 because step 5 is required to follow steps 2, 3 and 4.

If step 1 is to know, and step 2 is to reckon^1, and step 3 is to reckon^2, and step four is to yield, and step 5 is to enter the sphere of the spirit that activates new-man function, then yielding at step 4 cannot precede reckon^1 at step 2.

The conclusion: Since the old-man is reckoned dead at step 2, and the new-man is not accessed until step 5, it is impossible for the old-man or the new-man to have reckoned the old-man dead to sin. We must look elsewhere to discover who or what reckons the old-man dead to sin.

A Bit of Reasoning Amplified

1. Reckoning^1 the old-man dead to sin is step 2 in "Operation KRRY."

2. Reckoning^2 the new-man alive unto God is step 3 in "Operation KRRY."

3. Yielding to God the Holy Spirit is step 4 in "Operation KRRY."

4. Yielding to the Holy Spirit places the believer "in the Spirit."

5. When the believer is "in the Spirit," he is functioning from his new-man.

6. If the four steps in "Operation KRRY" are logical in order, and they are, then step 2 precedes step 4 and step 3 precedes step 4; therefore, if step 4 places the believer "in the Spirit," and the believer is functioning from the source of his new-man only when he is "in the Spirit," it cannot be the old-man or the new-man that reckons the old-man dead to sin because the step from which the believer functions from the new-man is two steps AFTER the old-man is reckoned[1] dead and one step AFTER the new-man is reckoned[2] alive.

Final Conclusions: It is the neutral soul, and more specifically the neutral self-consciousness, that reckons the old-man dead to sin and reckons the new-man alive unto God.

ADDENDUM #2

The following diagram is provided to show the relationship of the various facets of the soul to each other, and it traces the data being processed through the soul of a mature believer. This diagram is slide #8 that has been extracted from the PowerPoint presentation titled *Mentality of the Neutral Soul* developed by Rev. Darryl Anderson.

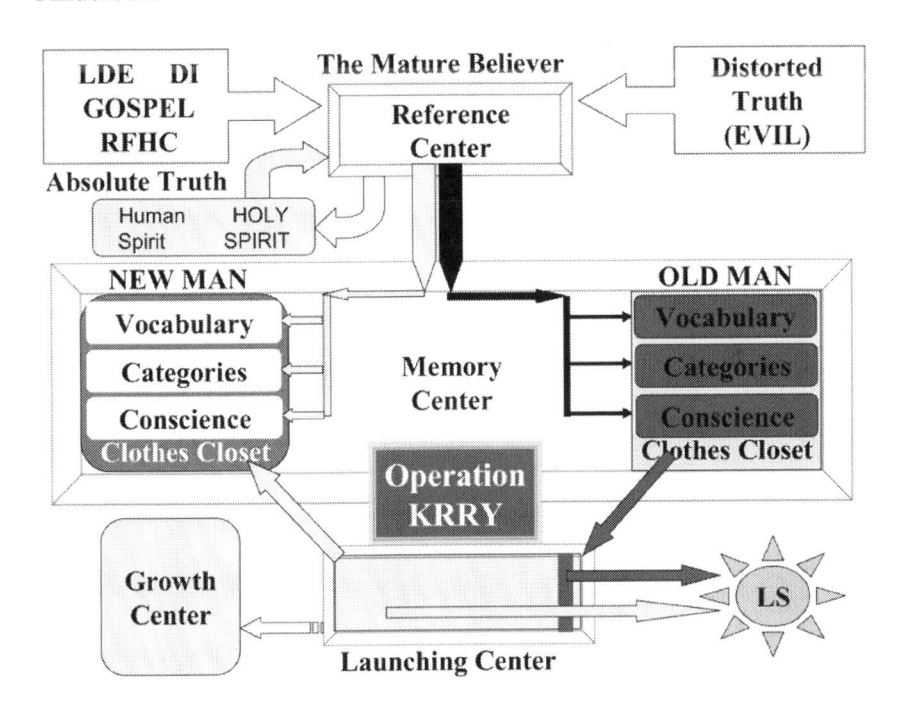

Legend:

LDE: laws of divine estanblishment
DI: four dvine institutions – freedom, marriage, family, nationalism
RHFC: royal family honor code
LS: life situation
Operation KRRY – (K)now, (R)eckon^1, (R)eckon^2, (Y)ield

Made in the USA
Columbia, SC
12 July 2024